We're from
Egypt

Victoria Parker

Welcome to Egypt!

Heinemann Library
Chicago, Illinois

Customer Service   888-454-2279
Visit our website at www.heinemannlibrary.com

Photo research by Maria Joannou
Photography by Roy Maconachie/EASI-Images
Designed by Ron Kamen and Celia Jones
Printed and bound in China by South China Printing Company

09 08 07 06 05
10 9 8 7 6 5 4 3 2 1

Library of Congress Cataloging-in-Publication Data
Parker, Victoria.
  We're from Egypt / Victoria Parker.
     p. cm.
  ISBN 1-4034-5783-2 (library binding) -- ISBN 1-4034-5790-5 (pbk.) 1. Egypt--Juvenile literature. I. Title.
DT49.P378 2005
962--dc22

                           2004017974

Acknowledgments
The author and publisher are grateful to the following for permission to reproduce copyright material:
Corbis/royalty Free pp. 4a. 4b. 30a; Getty Images/Photoshop p. 12; Oxford Scientific Films p. 30c; Roy Maconachie/EASI-Images pp. 1, 5, 6, 7a, 7b, 8a, 8b, 9, 10, 11, 13, 14a, 14b, 15a, 15b, 16, 17a, 17b, 18, 19a, 19b, 20a, 20b, 21a, 21b, 22a, 23, 24a, 24b, 25, 26a, 26b, 27a, 27b, 28a, 28b, 29, 30b.

Cover photograph of Karim, Heba and their friend, reproduced with permission of Roy Maconachie/EASI-Images. Many thanks to Karim, Ebtesam, Hamida and their families.

Every effort has been made to contact copyright holders of any material reproduced in this book. Any omissions will be rectified in subsequent printings if notice is given to the publisher. The paper used to print this book comes from sustainable resources.

Some words are shown in bold, **like this**. You can find out what they mean by looking in the glossary.

Contents

Where Is Egypt?

To learn about Egypt we meet three children who live there. Egypt is a big country in Africa. Most of the land is hot, dry **desert.**

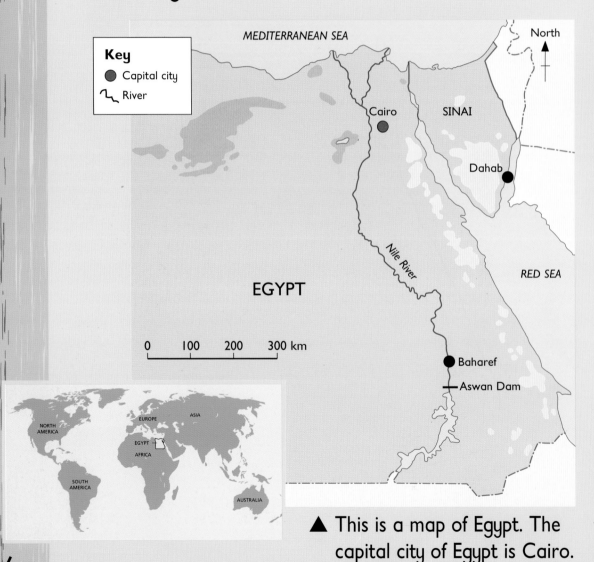

Key
- Capital city
- River

MEDITERRANEAN SEA

North

Cairo

SINAI

Dahab

Nile River

RED SEA

EGYPT

0   100   200   300 km

Baharef
Aswan Dam

NORTH AMERICA

EUROPE

ASIA

EGYPT

AFRICA

SOUTH AMERICA

AUSTRALIA

▲ This is a map of Egypt. The capital city of Egypt is Cairo.

The Nile River flows through Egypt. It runs from south to north. The land along the river is good for farming. This is where most Egyptians live.

▲ This Egyptian sailing boat is called a *felucca*.

Meet Karim

Karim is eight years old. He lives with his parents and his ten-year-old sister, Heba. Karim's father is a business person. His mother is a teacher.

Karim

Heba

Karim's mother

Karim's father

▲ Most people in Cairo, including Karim's family, live in apartment buildings.

The Nile River runs ▶ through Cairo.

Karim's family lives in Egypt's capital city, Cairo. Their home is on the first floor of a tall apartment building.

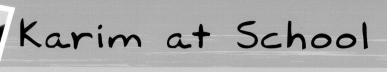

Karim at School

Karim and Heba go to school every day except Friday and Saturday. School starts at 8.00 A.M. It finishes at 4.00 P.M.

Karim's father drives ▶ them to school. Cairo has very busy roads.

There are 25 boys and girls in Karim's class. Karim has lessons in English and Arabic. Arabic is Egypt's main language.

▼ The boys and girls line up outside school at the start of the day.

Karim at Home

Karim enjoys Egyptian meals like bean stews, **kebabs,** and salads. He eats his food by scooping it up in bits of flat bread. The bread is called *khoubz*.

Karim's grandmother

▲ Karim's grandmother lives nearby and comes over for dinner sometimes.

◀ Karim likes roller-skating.

After dinner and homework, Karim and Heba play with their friends. They play in front of their apartment building. They like computer games and painting, too.

Egypt Long Ago

People lived in Egypt more than 5,000 years ago. They are known as the Ancient Egyptians. Their kings were called **pharaohs.** They built **pyramids** and statues.

▼ This is a huge Ancient Egyptian statue called the Great Sphinx.

pyramid

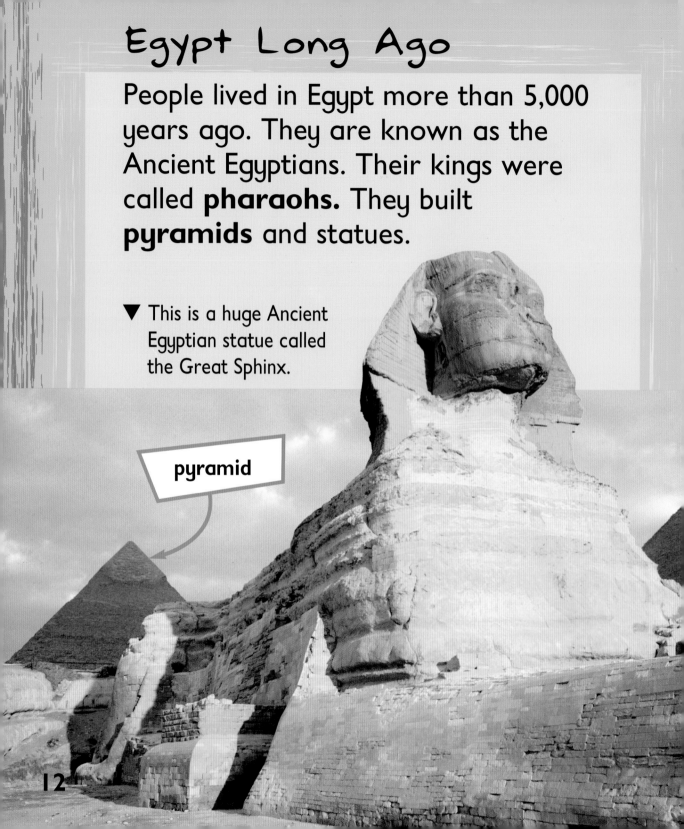

pyramid

Tourists come from all over the world to see the pyramids. The pyramids are where pharaohs were put when they died.

Meet Ebtesam

Ebtesam is six years old. She comes from Baharef. Baharef is a village in southern Egypt where people farm **dates.** She lives with her parents and her older brother, Mohamed.

Ebtesam

Mohamed

Ebtesam's father

Ebtesam's mother

▲ Ebtesam's village is on the edge of the **desert.**

Ebtesam's uncles, aunts and cousins live in the same village. Everyone in the village has a house with a flat roof. They can dry dates in the sun on their roof.

Date Harvesting

Ebtesam's family does not have enough money to buy modern farming **equipment.** They do all the jobs on their farm using simple tools. It is very hard work.

Mohamed climbs tall palm trees
▼ to pick the **dates.**

Ebtesam's family sells ▶
their dates at a
market like this one.

Ebtesam helps by carrying baskets full
of juicy dates. The family works
together to take the fruits off the
branches and to sort them.

17

Ebtesam's Day

In the mornings, Ebtesam does her jobs on the farm. Her family plants vegetables to eat and grows **dates** to make money. They keep chickens, too.

▲ One vegetable they grow is called *molokiyya*. It is a bit like spinach.

▲ Ebtesam's school has
a yard for the children
to play in.

Some children go to school for the
morning. Ebtesam and her friends go
to school in the afternoon. She has
two hours of homework every day.

19

Ebtesam's Home

Ebtesam's home has **electricity** but no running water. Ebtesam gets all the water for the family from the village pump.

◀ Getting water from the pump is hard work!

Ebtesam's family sits on the floor to eat. Sometimes they cook on a small heater in the kitchen. Other times, they cook over an outside fire.

21

Weather and Water

It does not rain very often in Egypt. Farmers have to use water from the Nile River to help their crops grow.

Sometimes farmers ▶ use donkeys to help move water to their fields.

About 50 years ago, a huge **dam** was built on the Nile River at Aswan. The dam collects water from the river. People can use it to water their crops.

▲ The dam slows the river's flow, and makes a lake behind it.

Meet Hamida

Hamida is six years old. She lives with her parents and sister, Sara. They have a house in a town called Dahab in the Sinai **Desert.**

Hamida's father

Hamida's mother

Sara

Hamida

◀ Dahab is a long way from the Nile River.

Hamida's family are **Bedouins.** Bedouin people **traditionally** live in tents. Hamida's family often goes to stay at a Bedouin camp in the desert mountains.

▼ Hamida's family has lots of friends at the mountain camp.

Hamida Helps Out

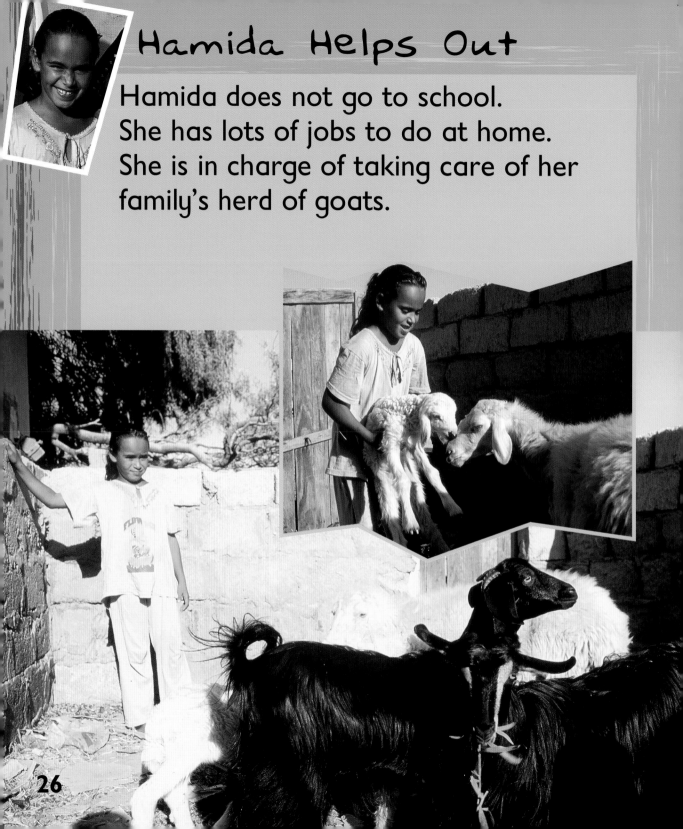

Hamida does not go to school.
She has lots of jobs to do at home.
She is in charge of taking care of her
family's herd of goats.

Hamida also helps her parents with the cooking. Hamida's father makes some very tasty bread!

The bread is baked and eaten with vegetables. ▶

27

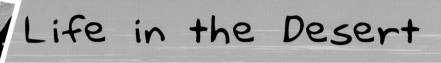

Life in the Desert

Many tourists visit the Sinai Desert. They often pay to visit the **Bedouin** camp. Hamida and her mother make bracelets and crafts to sell.

▼ Many Bedouins keep camels. Camels are good at walking on desert sand.

Hamida's father earns money by taking the tourists on trips in the **desert**. Bedouins know all about desert animals and plants and where to find water.

Egyptian Fact File

Flag

Capital City

Cairo

Money

Pounds and piastres

Religion
• Most people in Egypt are Muslims. There are some Christians, too.

Language
• The main language of Egypt is Arabic. Many people also speak English, and some speak French.

Try speaking Egyptian Arabic!

salaam aleikum......................*hello*

izzayak.................................*how are you?*

shukran................................*thank you*

Glossary

Bedouin an old tribe (group of people) who live in tents in the desert. They often move around rather than living in one place.

dam wall built across a river to make a huge lake behind it

date fruit that grows on palm trees

desert very hot, dry area of land that has almost no rain and very few plants

electricity power used for heating, lighting, and running equipment

equipment tools and machines that help people do a job

kebab type of grilled sausage or meat

pharaoh king who ruled Ancient Egypt

pyramid huge stone building in the desert, where dead pharaohs were buried

tradition something that has been going for a very long time without changing

More Books to Read

Foster, Leila and Fox, Mary. *Continents: Africa*. Chicago: Heinemann Library, 2002.

Pyers, Greg. *Habitat Explorer: Desert Explorer*. Chicago: Raintree, 2004.

Gibbons, Gail. *Mummies, Pyramids and Pharaohs*. New York: Little Brown and Company, 2004.

Index